How to draw airplanes trains and ships

How to draw airplanes, trains and ships

This book belongs to:

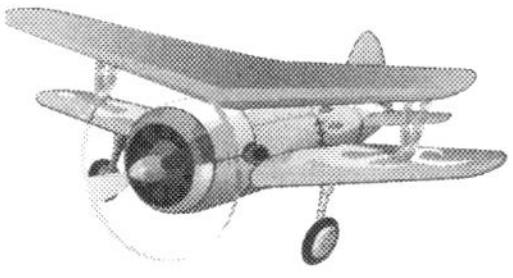

Let`s learn how to draw

We will learn how to draw in a simple but efficient way by using the grid method.

The grid method of drawing gives you the opportunity to produce an accurate line drawing by reducing your subject to a series of small squares.

But, as a first step, grab a sharpened pencil, a good eraser and be ready to start an amazing drawing adventure.

Grid copy method

The grid copy method splits your entire subject into smaller squares allowing you to focus on one square at a time. It is recommended to begin with grid box A1 to grid box F7, until your full image has been drawn.

Start here

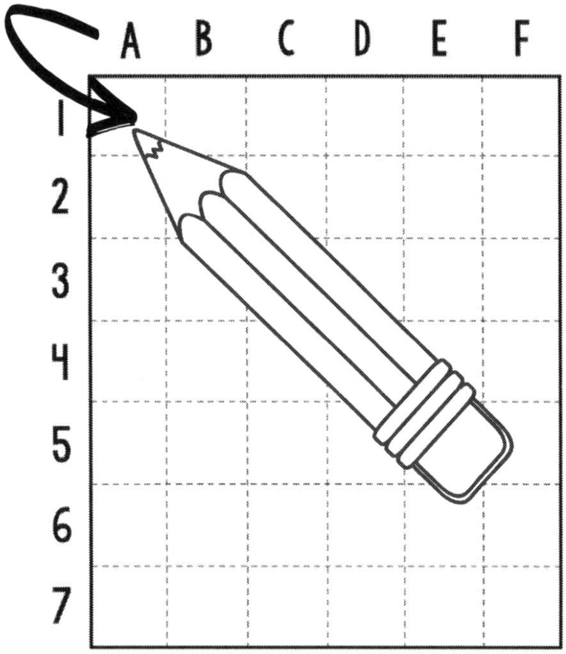

Focus on one square at a time

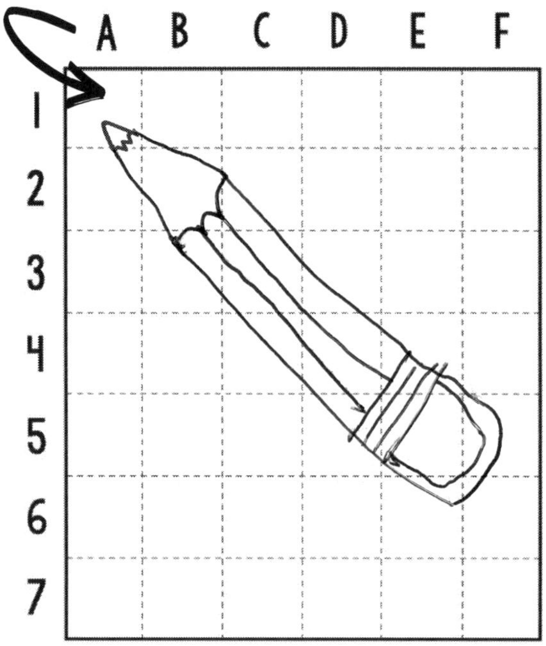

Let`s start with another step-by-step example of how to draw a airplane. As we mentioned before, we recommend starting from grid box A1 to grid box F7 (from the left to the right / from top to bottom)

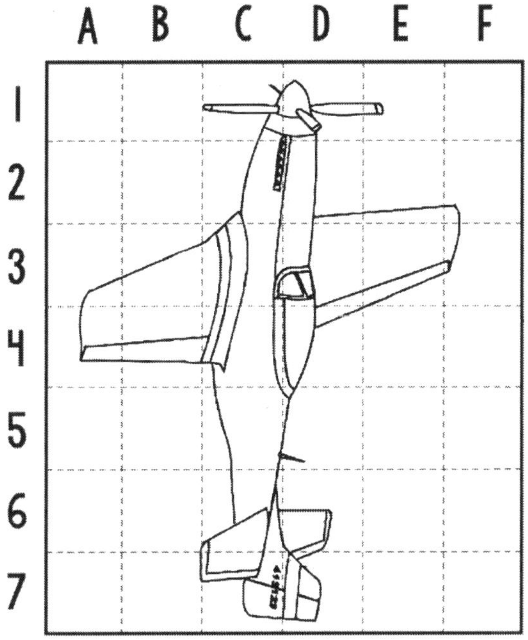

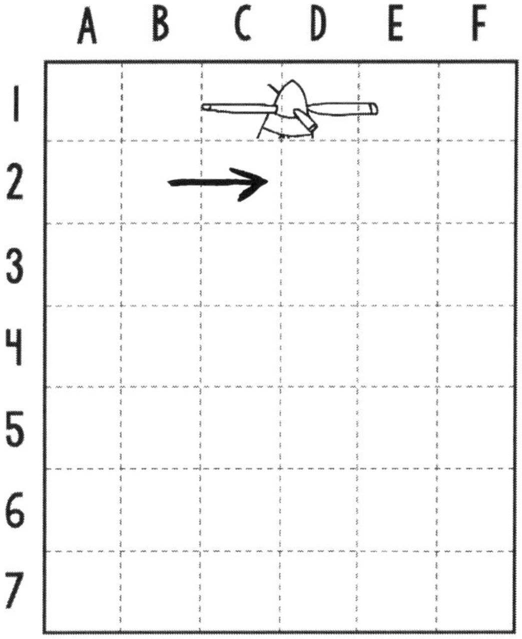

The first squares to focus on are C1, D1 and E1 in this order. After we finished line 1, we start to draw all the squares from line 2, from left to right, and so on.

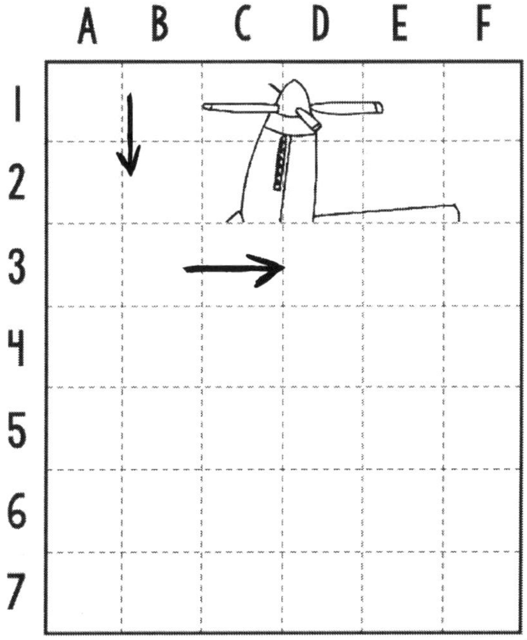

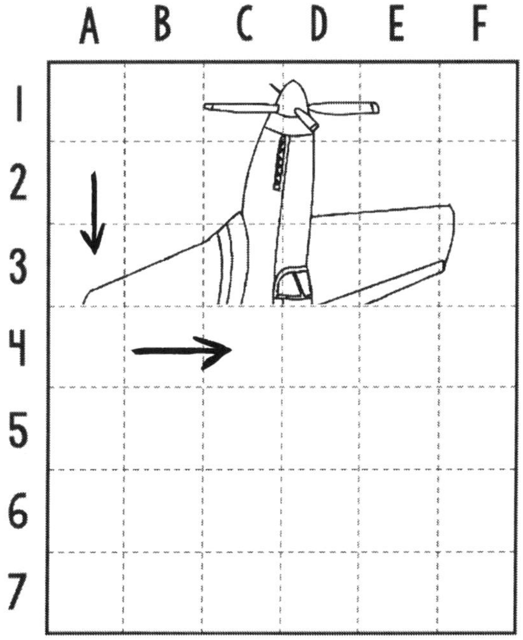

Following these recommendations, we reached line 4 and elements of our drawing begin to take shape.

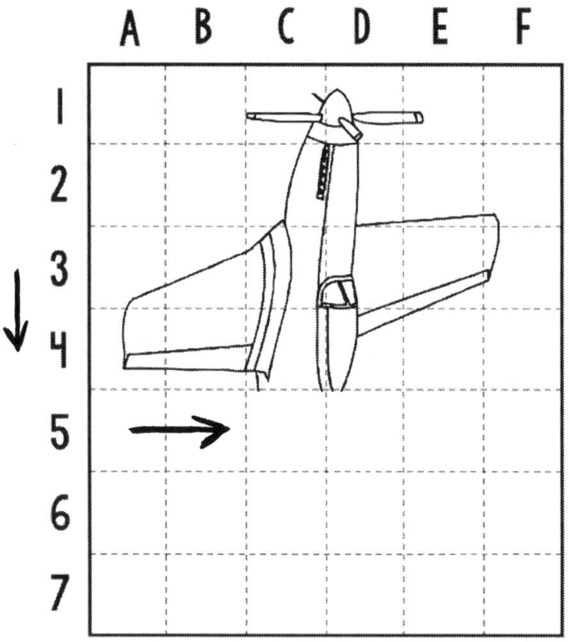

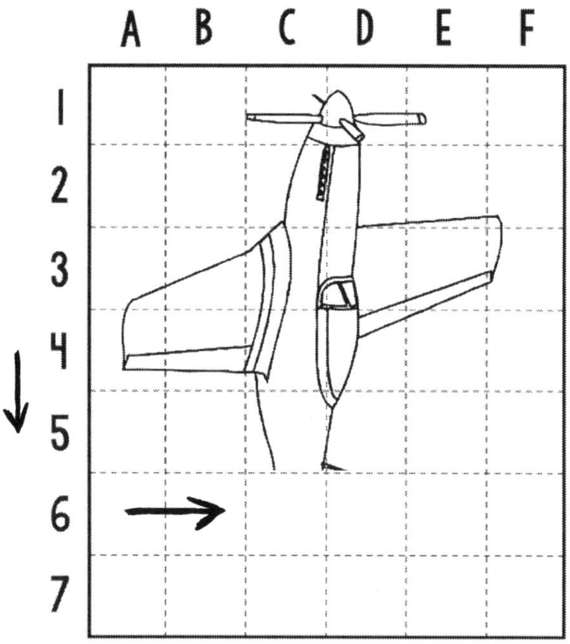

Finally, our image comes to an end by reaching line 7. We are very confident that your next drawings will be more and more beautiful and accurate.

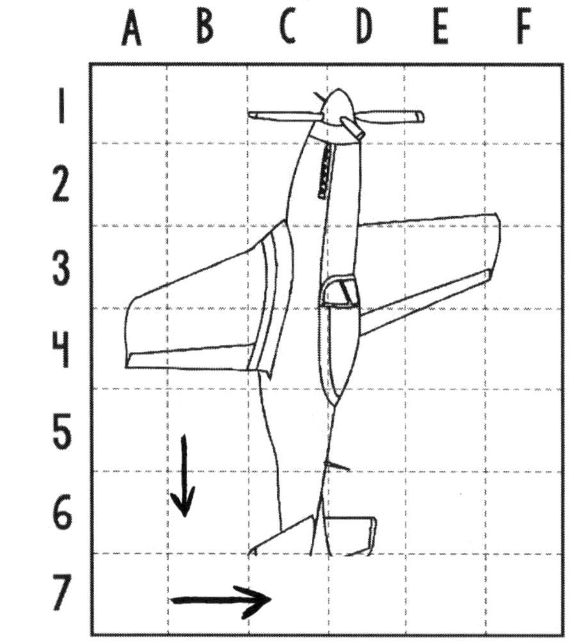

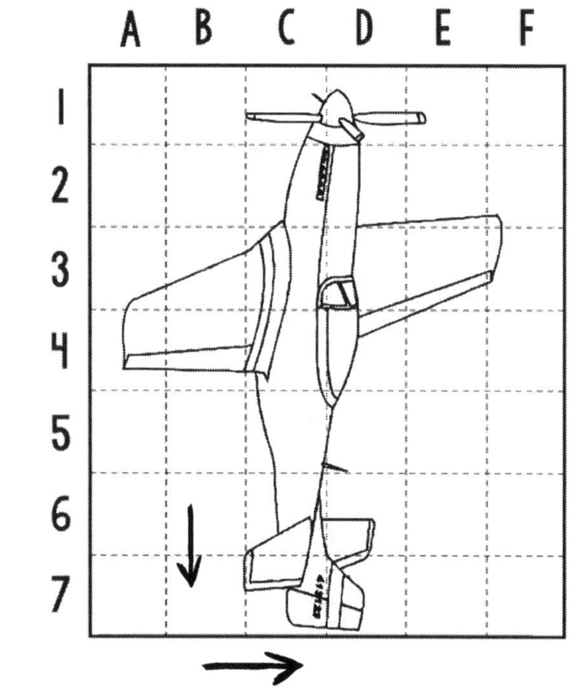

Do not hurry, take all the time you need and be focused on every single square

Start gradually with the most simple lines and shapes in the square

Practice again and again and your drawings will be more and more beautiful

And the most important...

Enjoy your draw adventure!

AIRPLANE

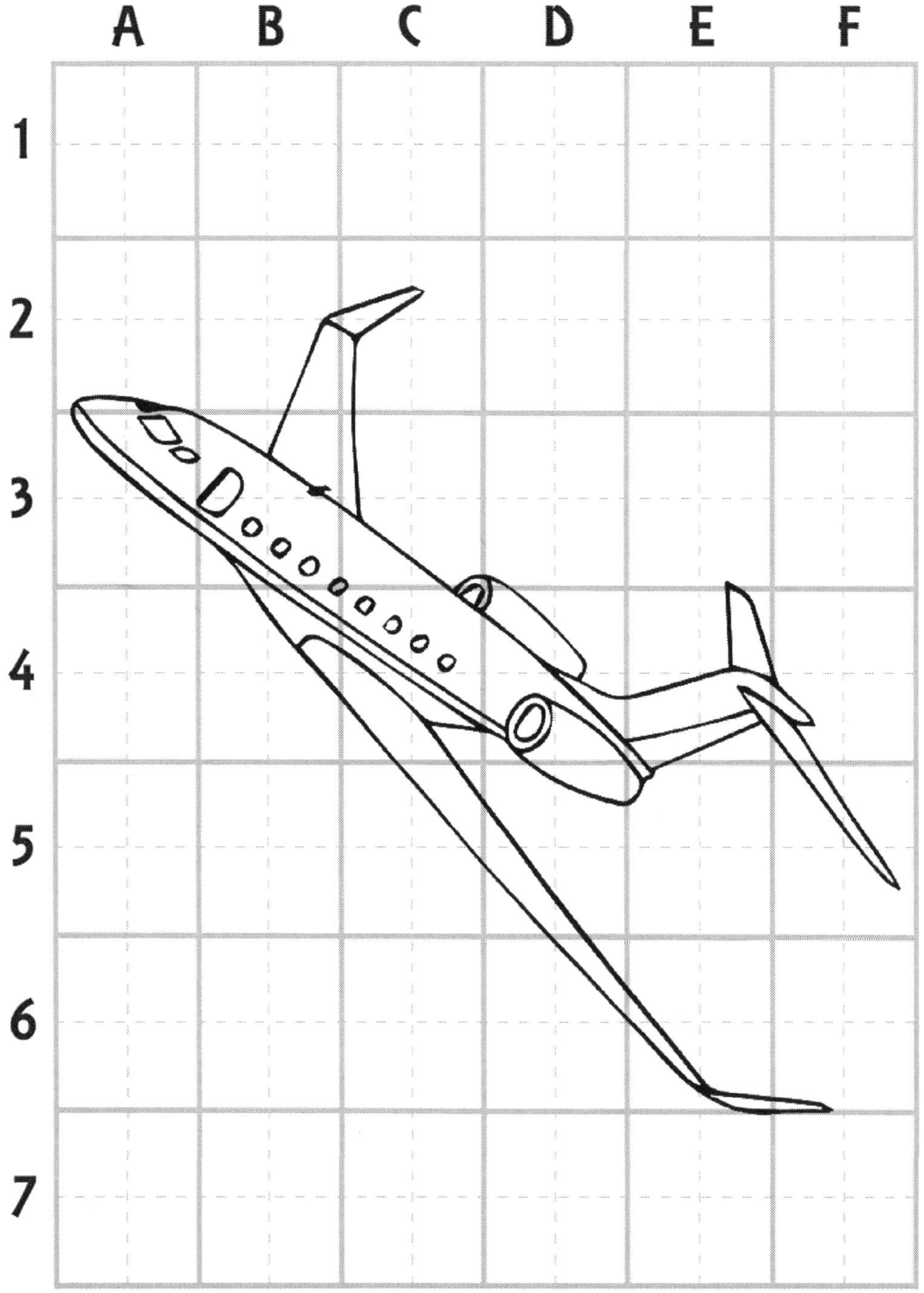
A
B
C
D
E
F
1
2
3
4
5
6
7

	A	B	C	D	E	F
1						
2						
3						
4						
5						
6						
7						

AIRPLANE

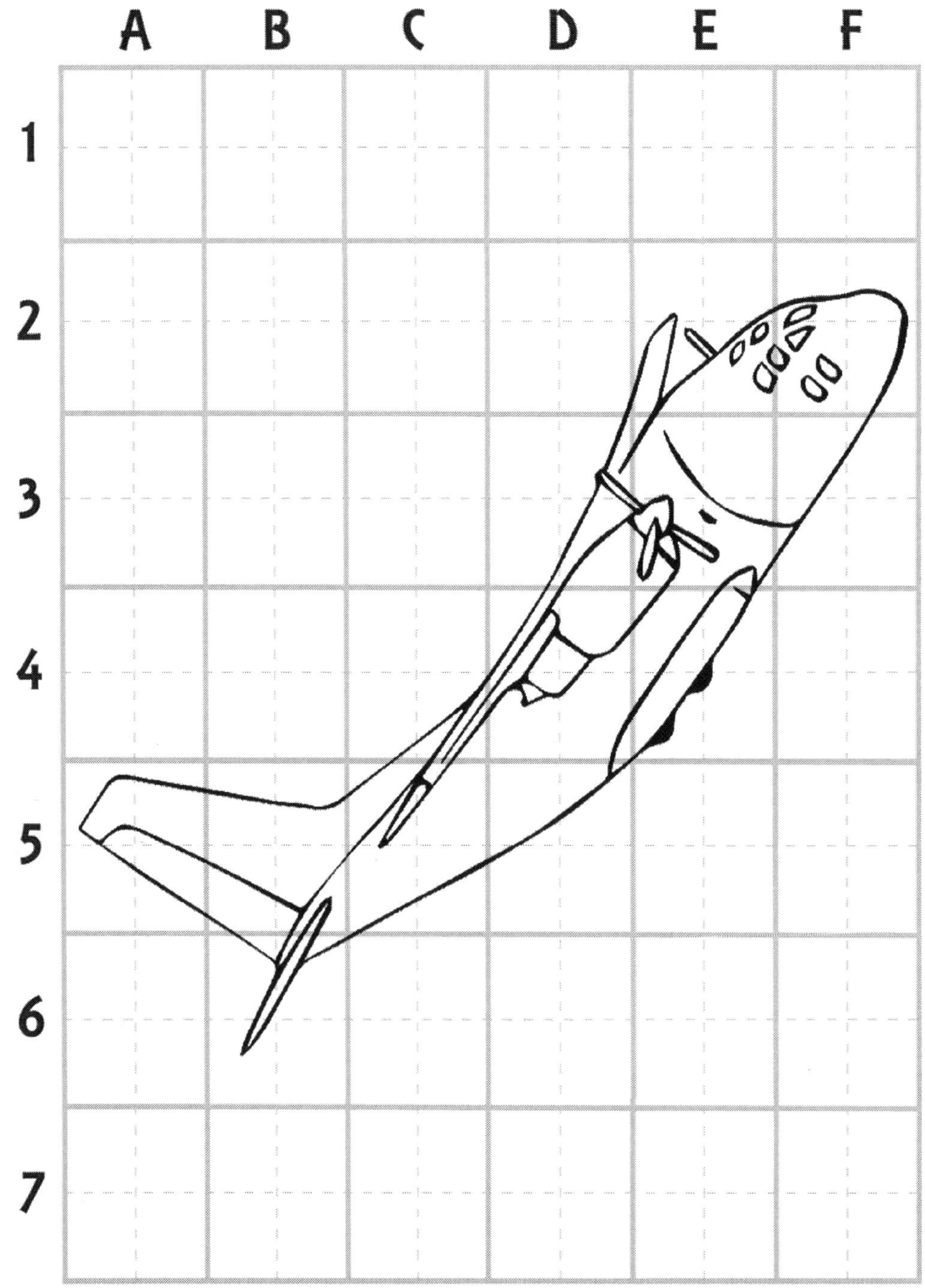
A
B
C
D
E
F
1
2
3
4
5
6
7

	A	B	C	D	E	F
1						
2						
3						
4						
5						
6						
7						

TRAINS

	A	B	C	D	E	F
1						
2						
3						
4						
5						
6						
7						

SHIPS

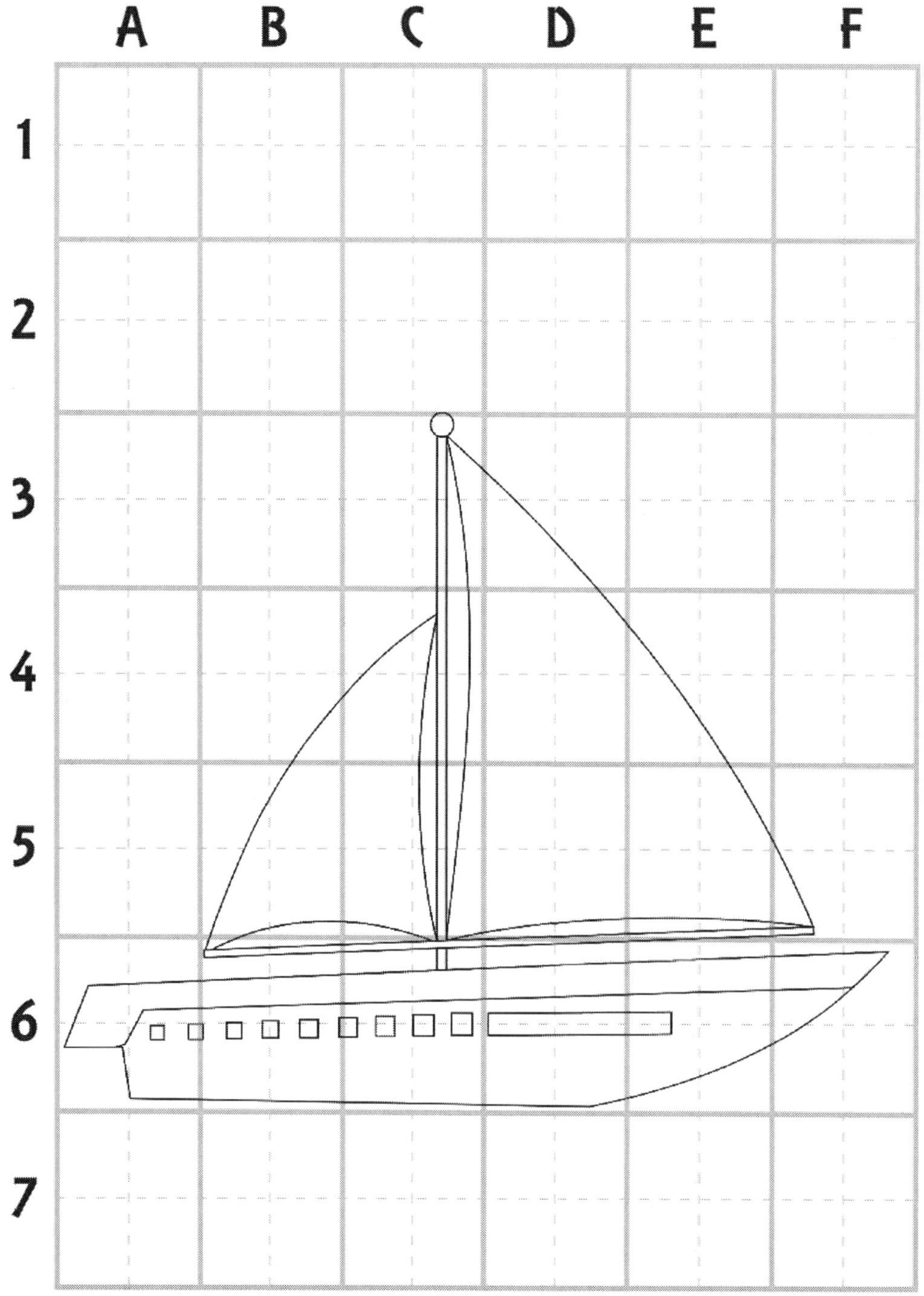
A
B
C
D
E
F
1
2
3
4
5
6
7

	A	B	C	D	E	F
1						
2						
3						
4						
5						
6						
7						

AIRPLANE

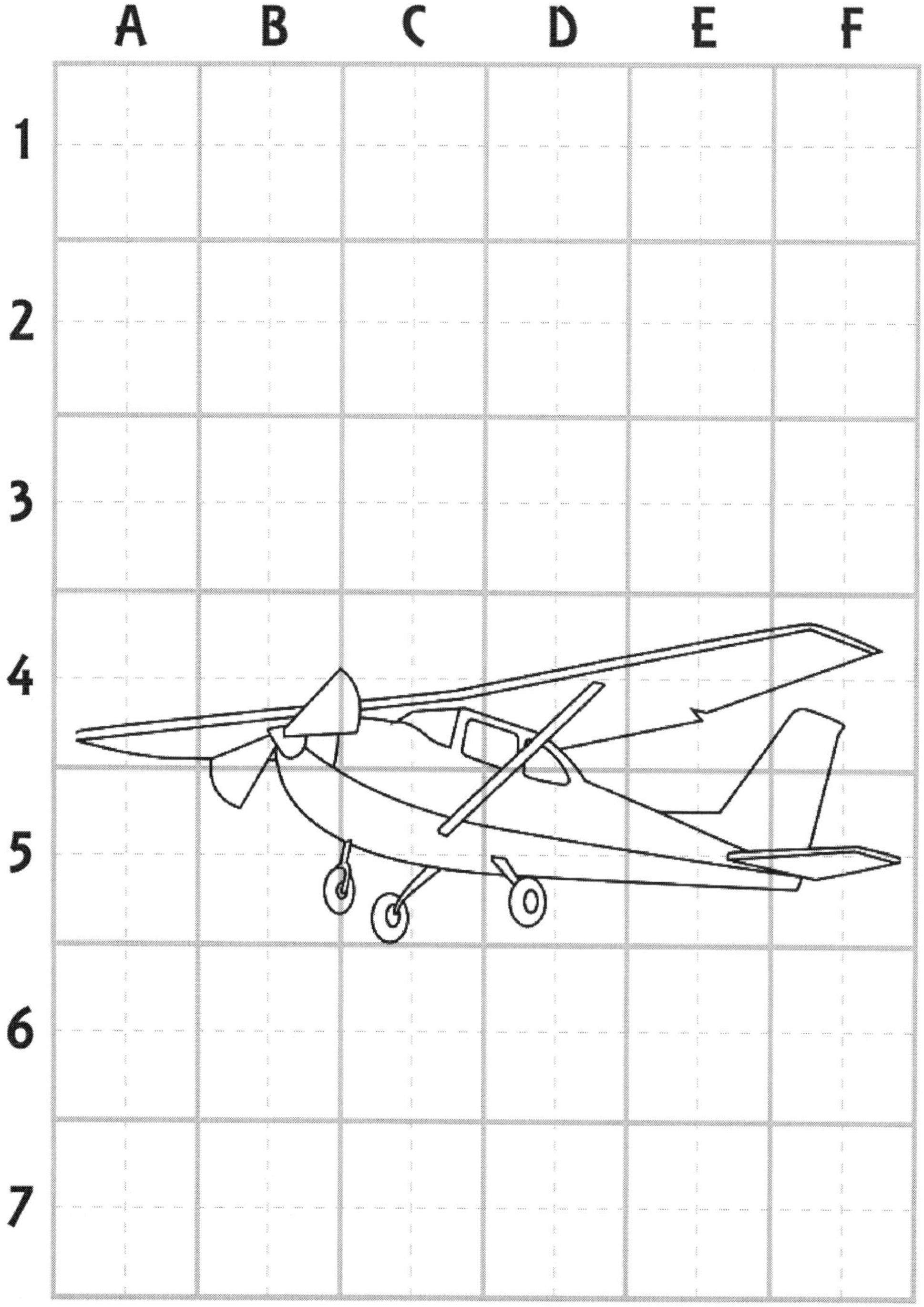
A
B
C
D
E
F
1
2
3
4
5
6
7

	A	B	C	D	E	F
1						
2						
3						
4						
5						
6						
7						

TRAINS

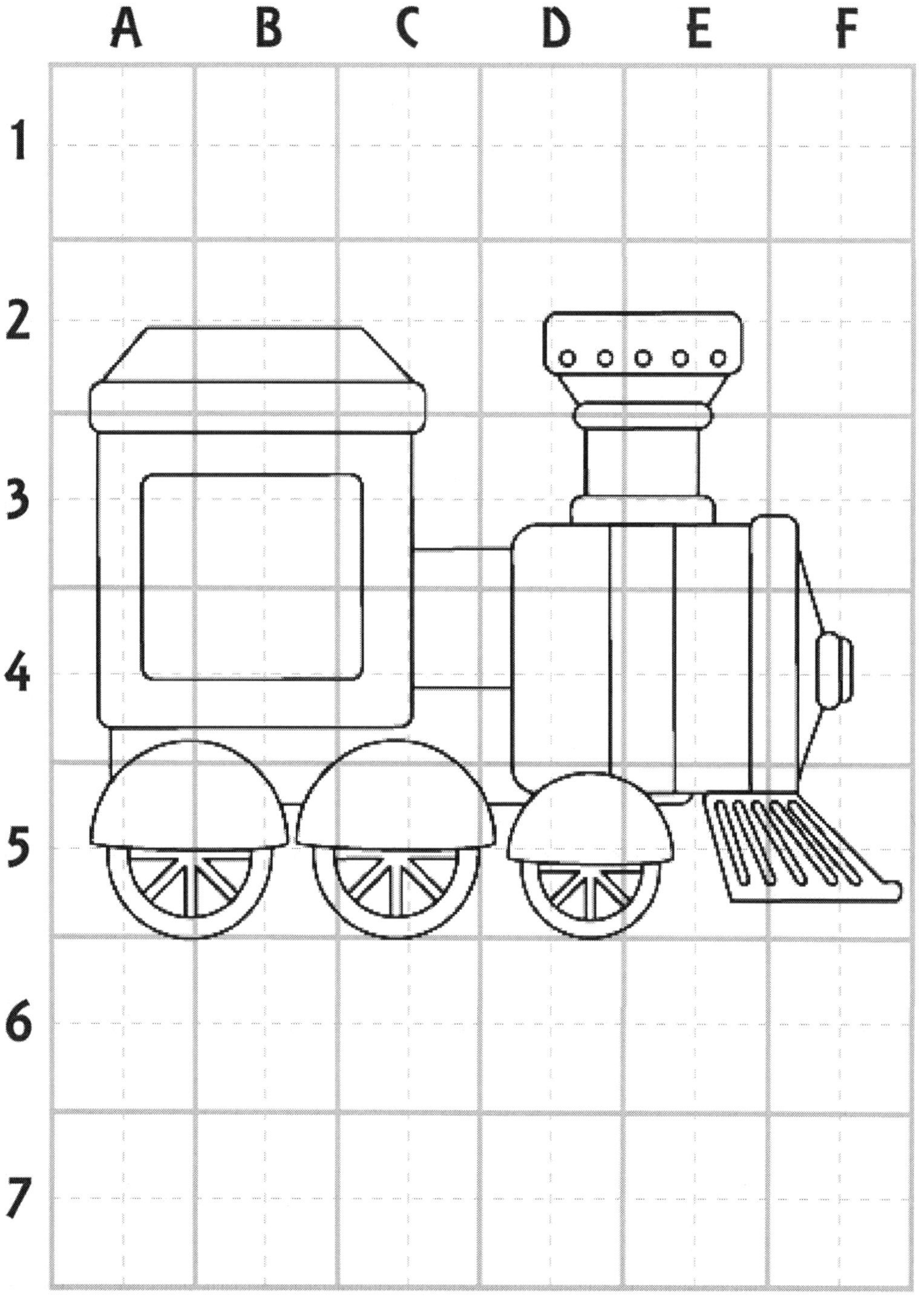
A
B
C
D
E
F
1
2
3
4
5
6
7

	A	B	C	D	E	F
1						
2						
3						
4						
5						
6						
7						

SHIPS

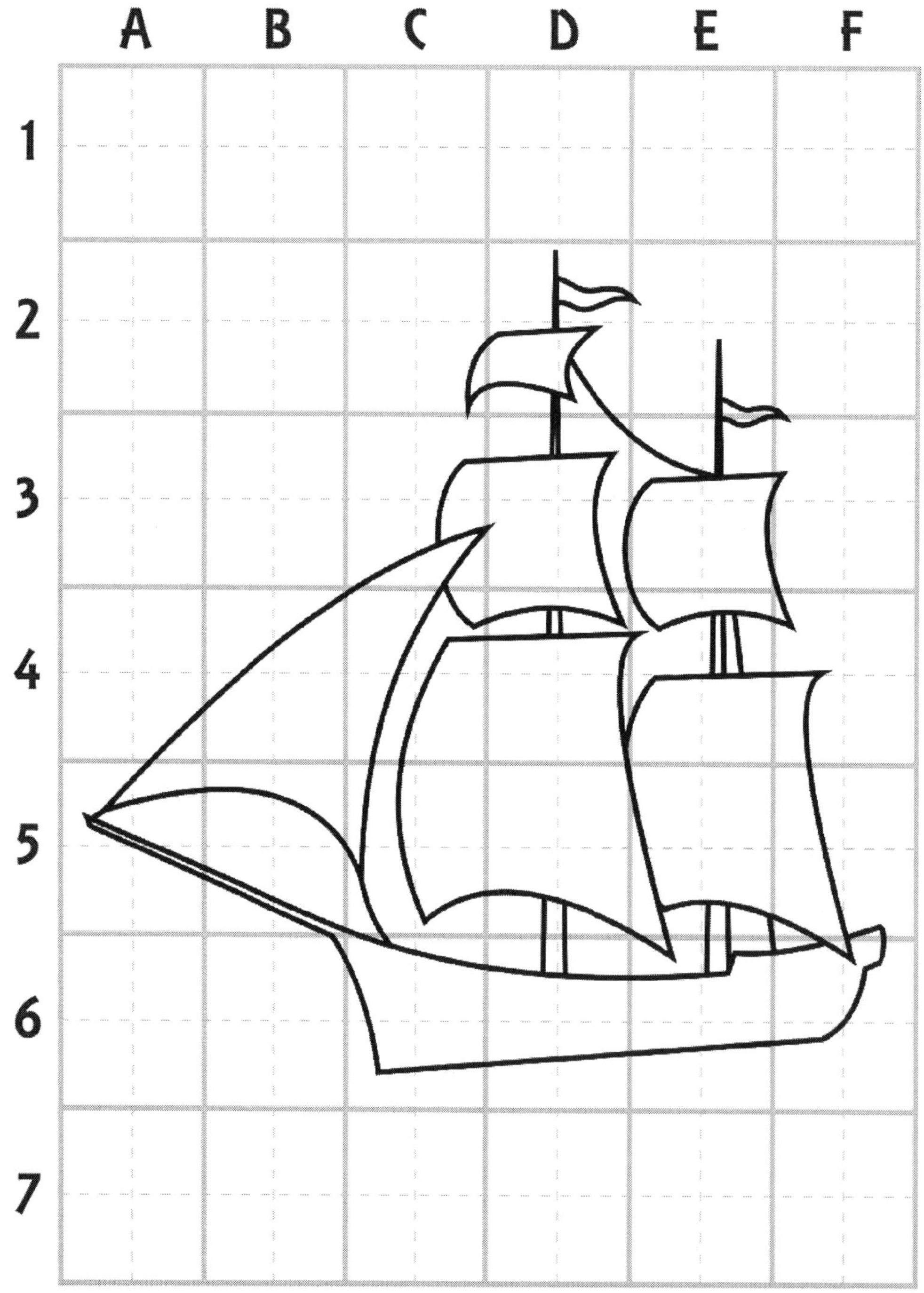
A B C D E F
1
2
3
4
5
6
7

	A	B	C	D	E	F
1						
2						
3						
4						
5						
6						
7						

AIRPLANE

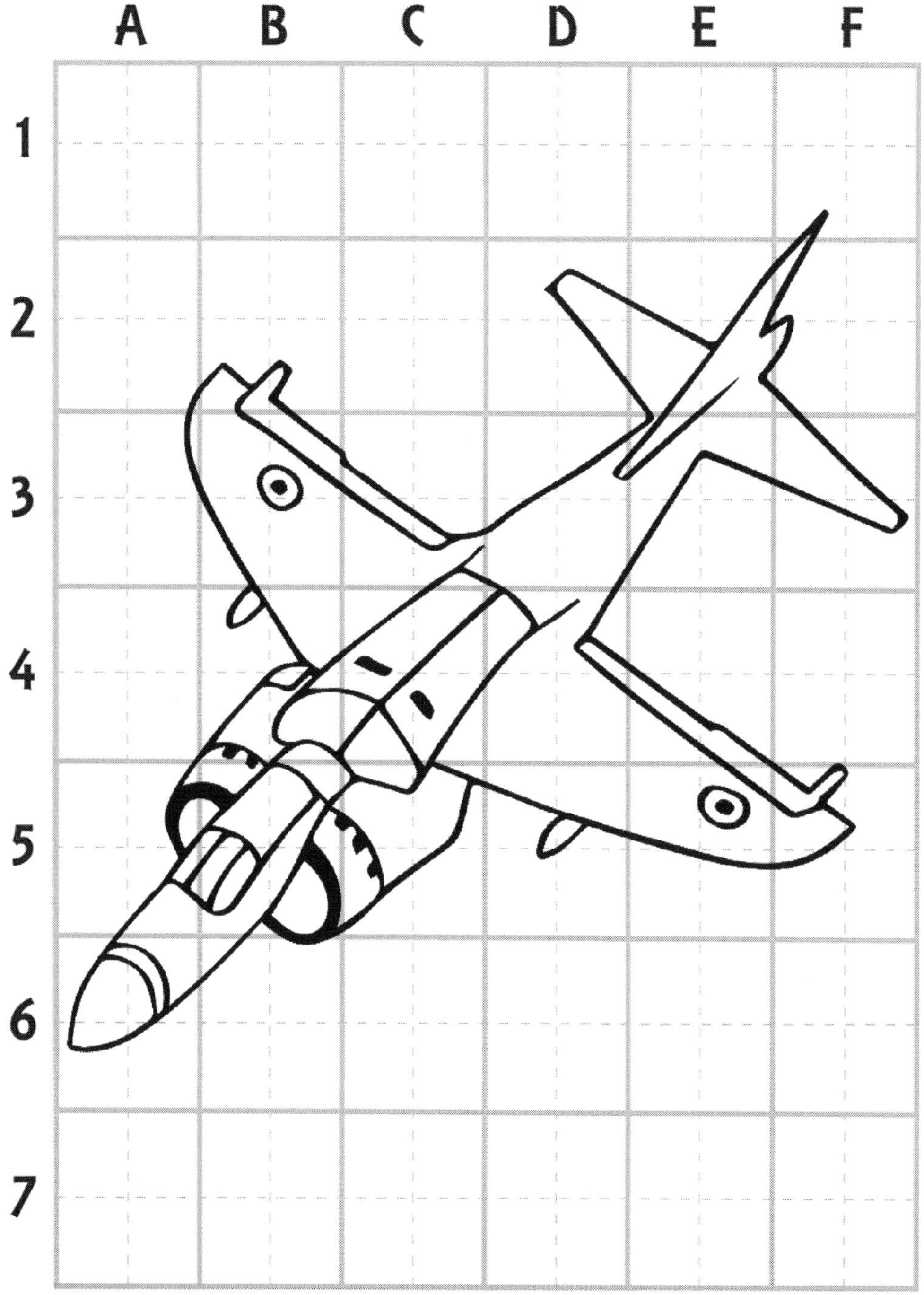
A B C D E F
1
2
3
4
5
6
7

	A	B	C	D	E	F
1						
2						
3						
4						
5						
6						
7						

TRAINS

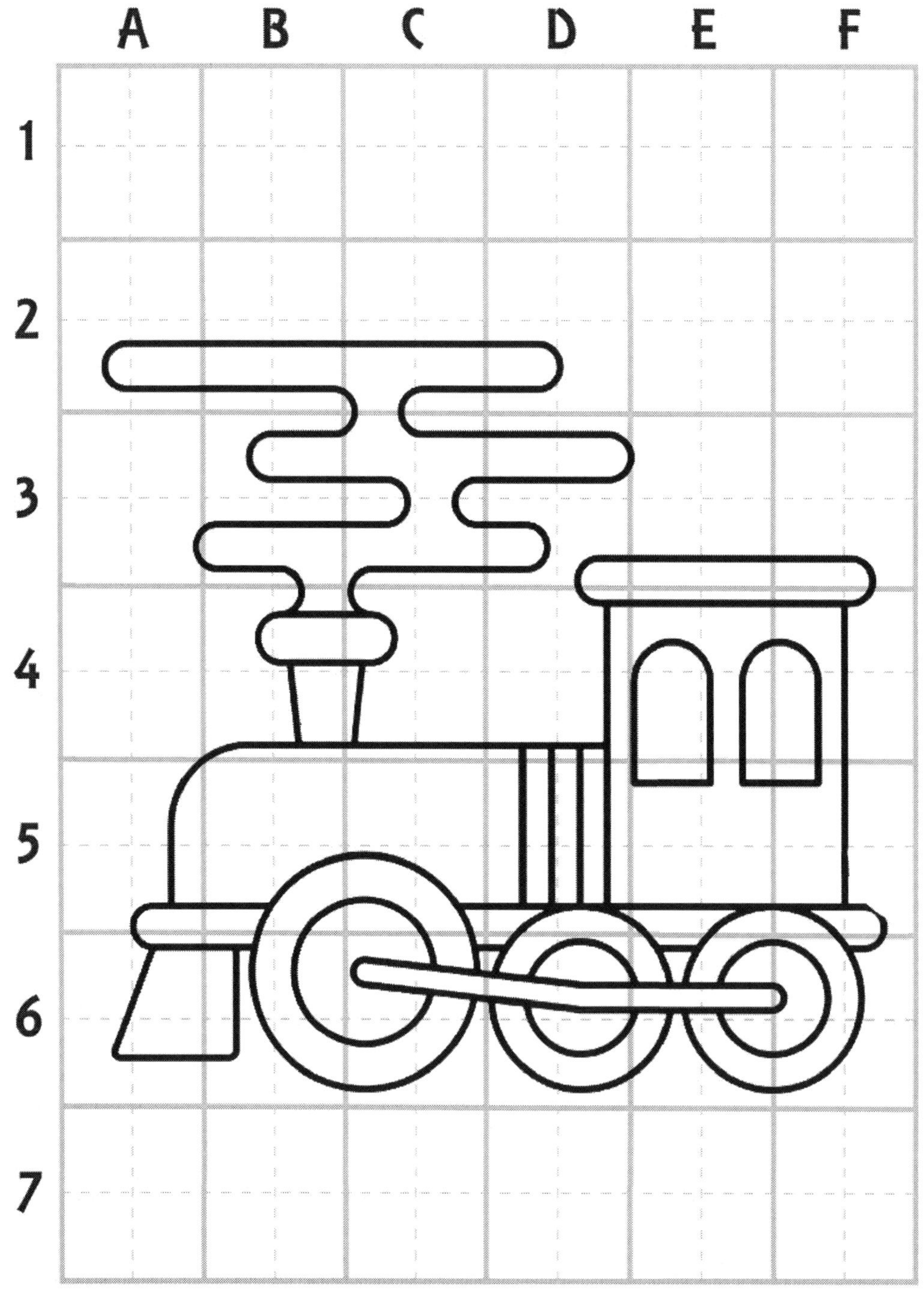

	A	B	C	D	E	F
1						
2						
3						
4						
5						
6						
7						

SHIPS

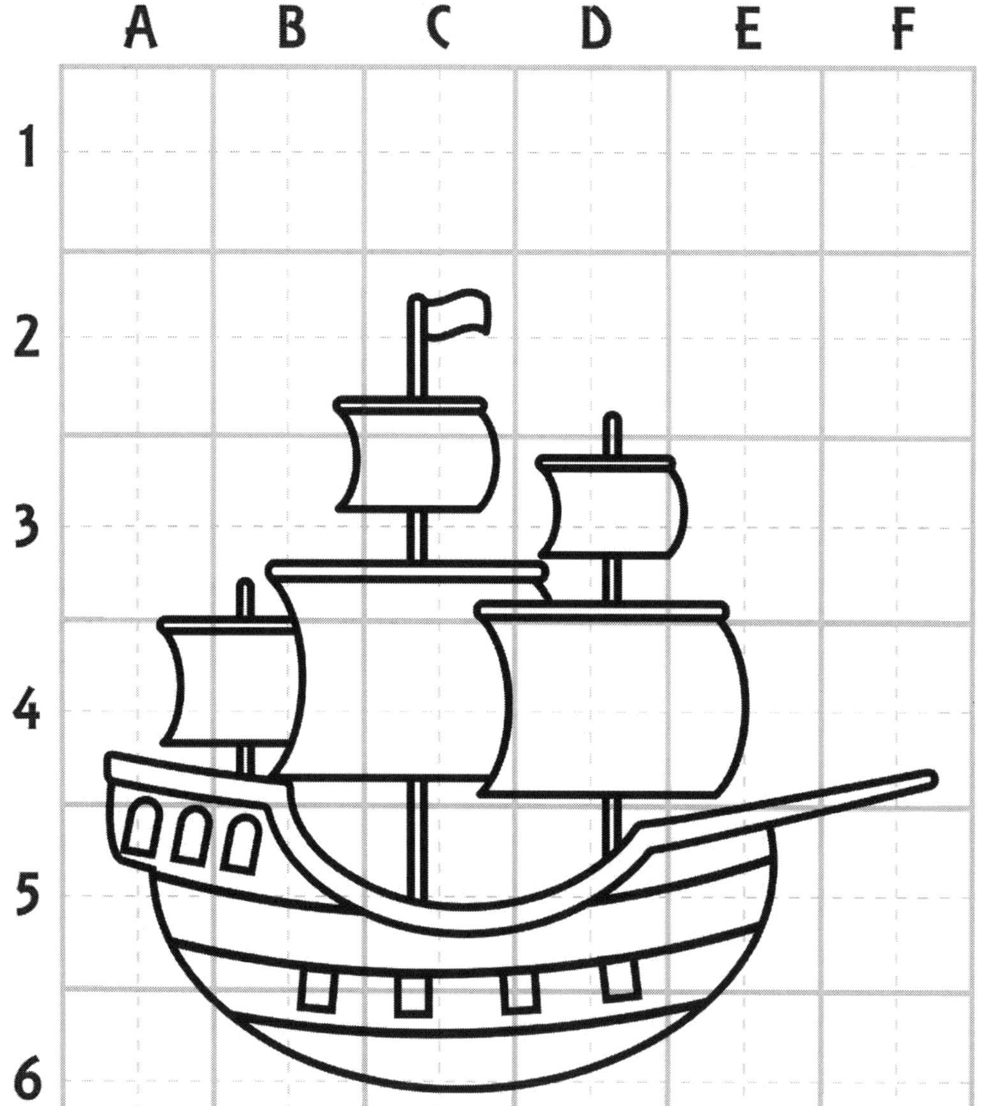
A
B
C
D
E
F
1
2
3
4
5
6
7

	A	B	C	D	E	F
1						
2						
3						
4						
5						
6						
7						

AIRPLANE

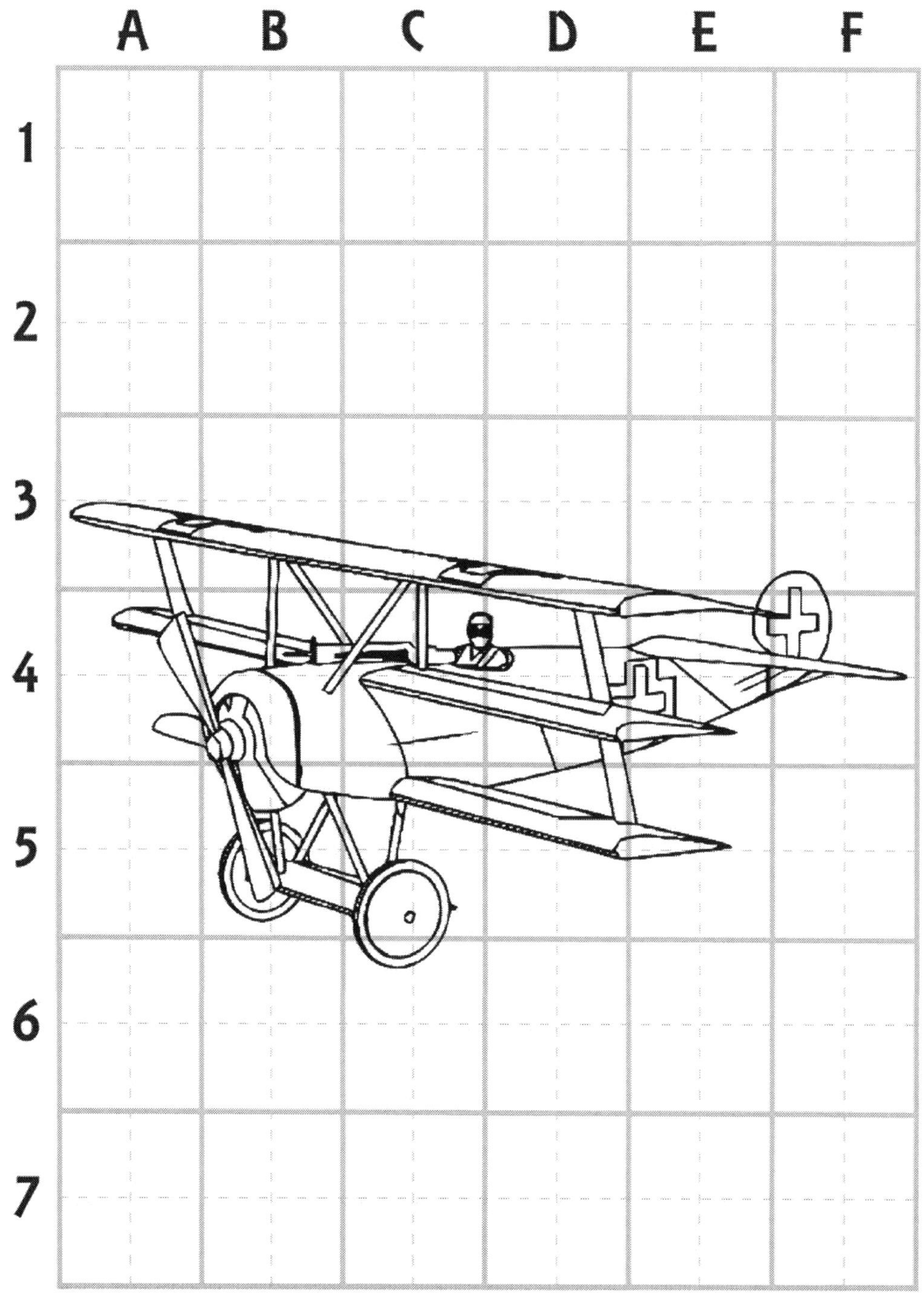
A B C D E F
1 2 3 4 5 6 7

	A	B	C	D	E	F
1						
2						
3						
4						
5						
6						
7						

TRAINS

A
B
C
D
E
F
1
2
3
4
5
6
7

	A	B	C	D	E	F
1						
2						
3						
4						
5						
6						
7						

SHIPS

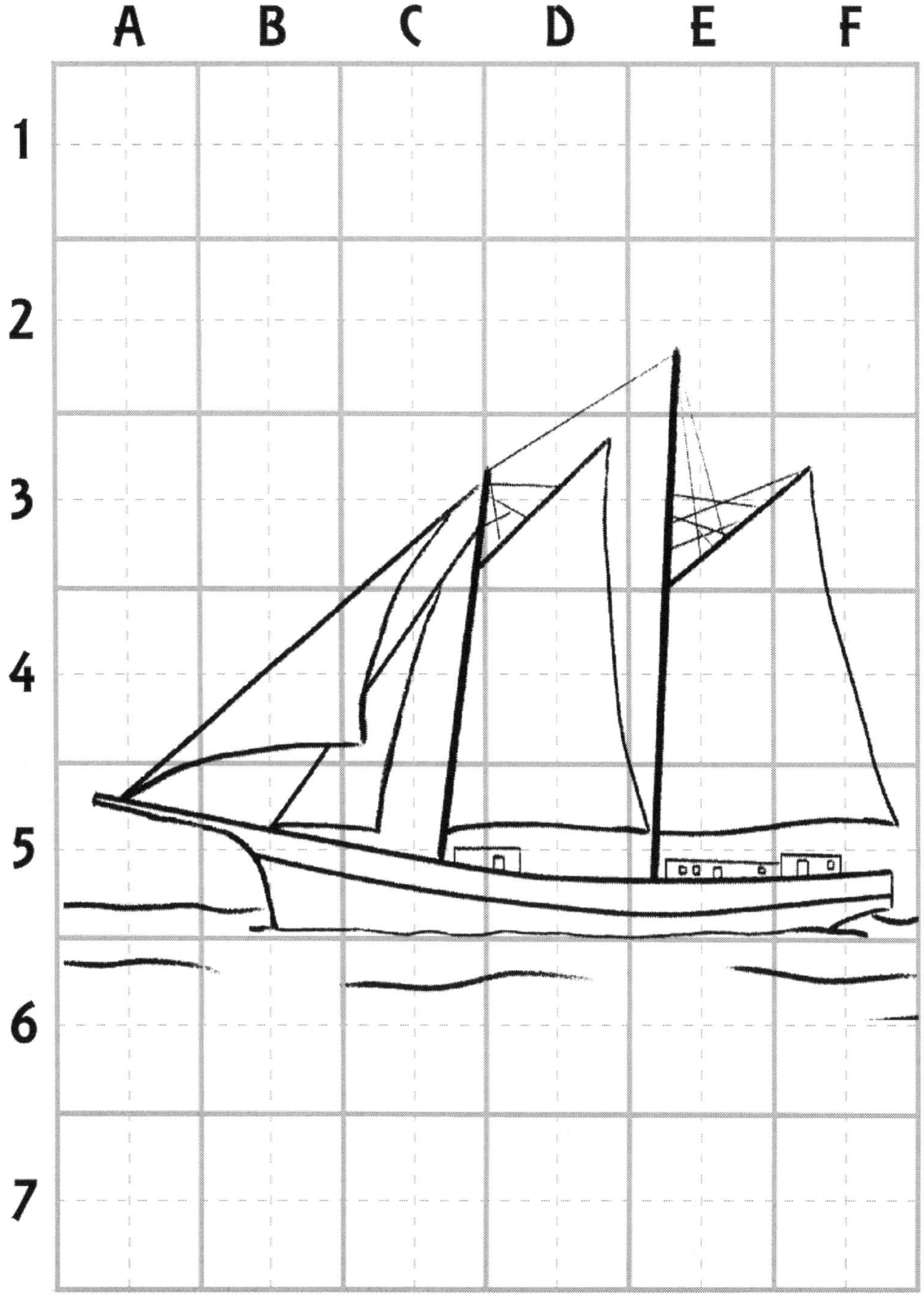
A B C D E F
1
2
3
4
5
6
7

	A	B	C	D	E	F
1						
2						
3						
4						
5						
6						
7						

AIRPLANE

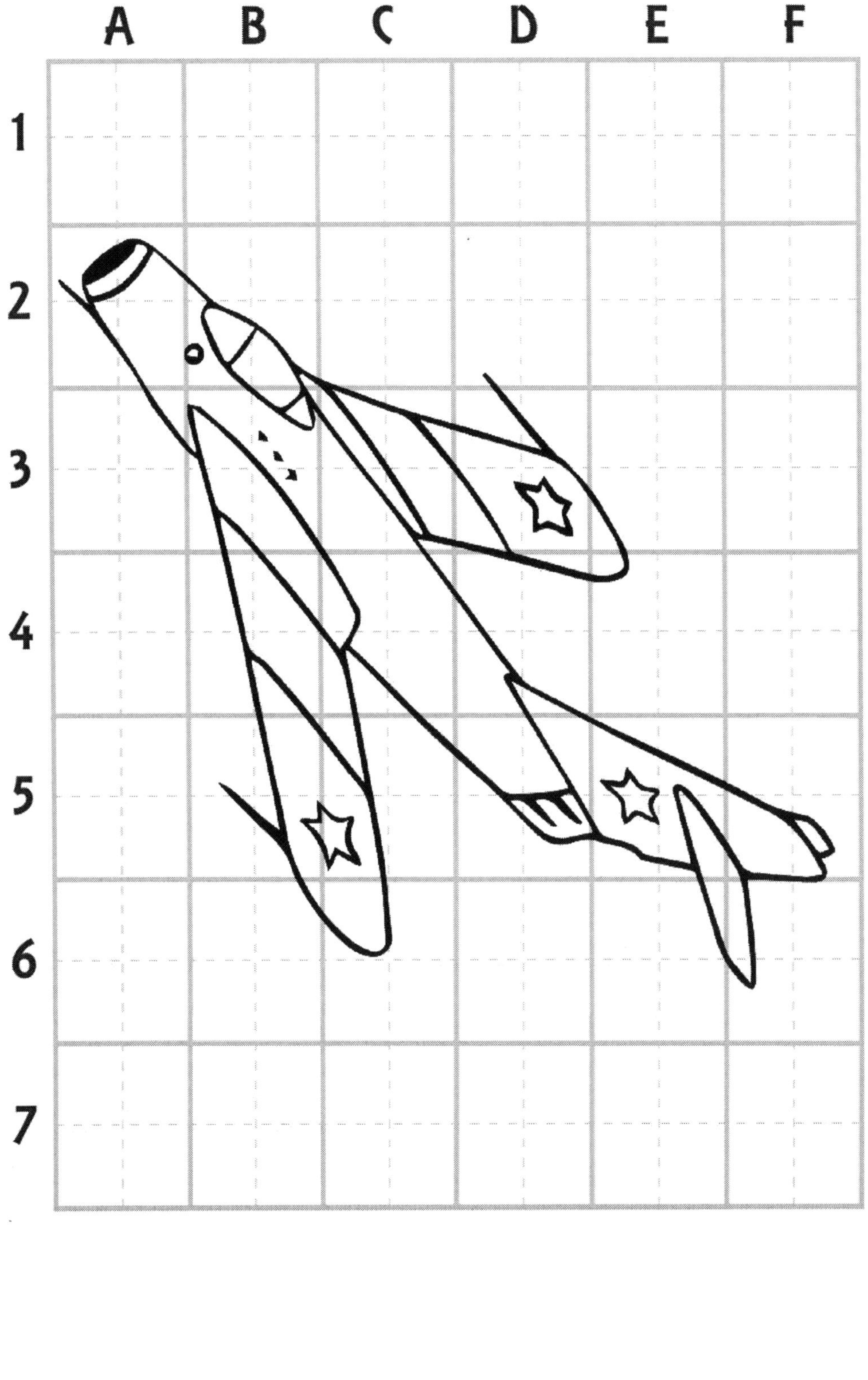
A B C D E F
1
2
3
4
5
6
7

	A	B	C	D	E	F
1						
2						
3						
4						
5						
6						
7						

TRAINS

A
B
C
D
E
F
1
2
3
4
5
6
7

	A	B	C	D	E	F
1						
2						
3						
4						
5						
6						
7						

SHIPS

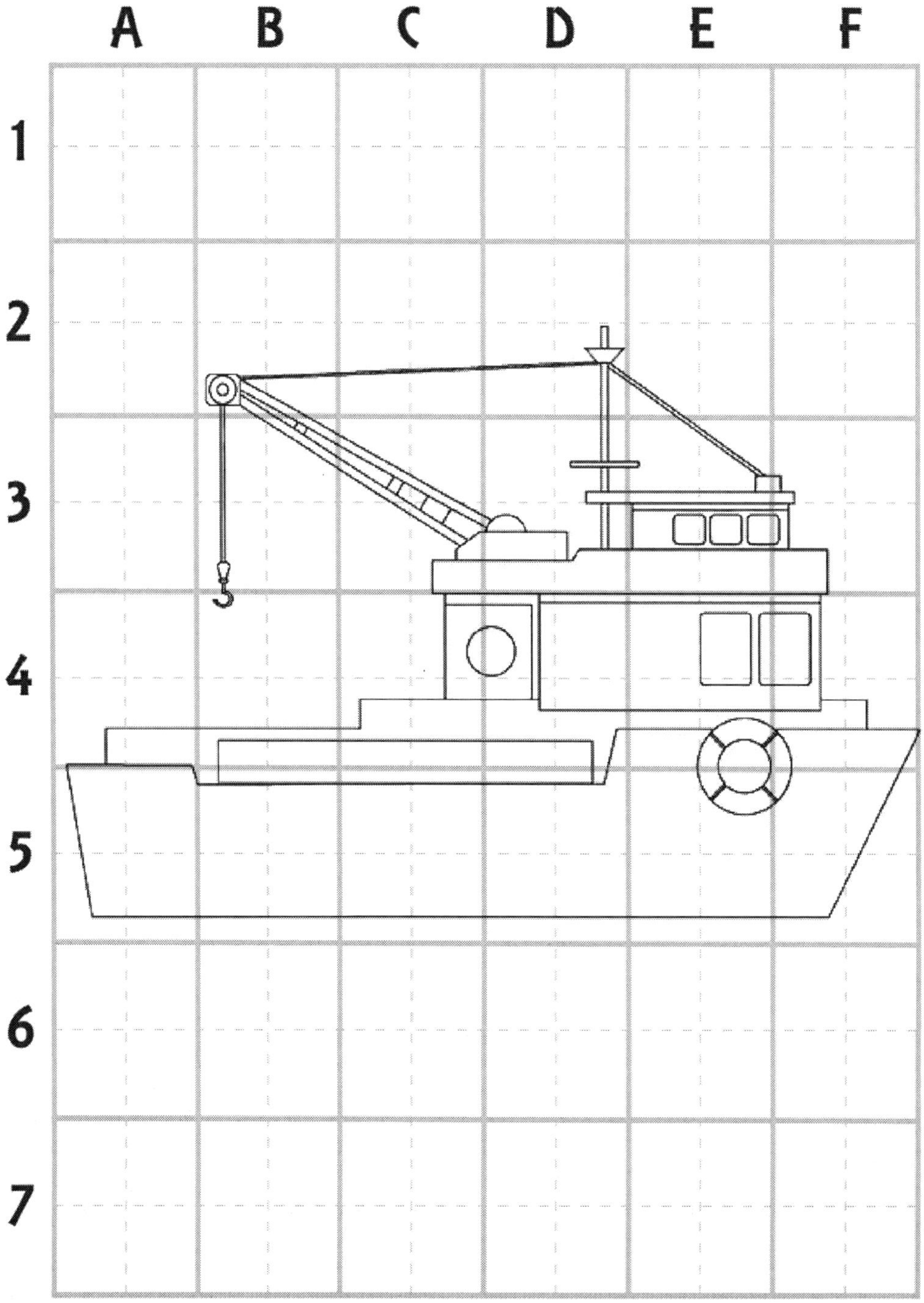
A
B
C
D
E
F
1
2
3
4
5
6
7

	A	B	C	D	E	F
1						
2						
3						
4						
5						
6						
7						

AIRPLANE

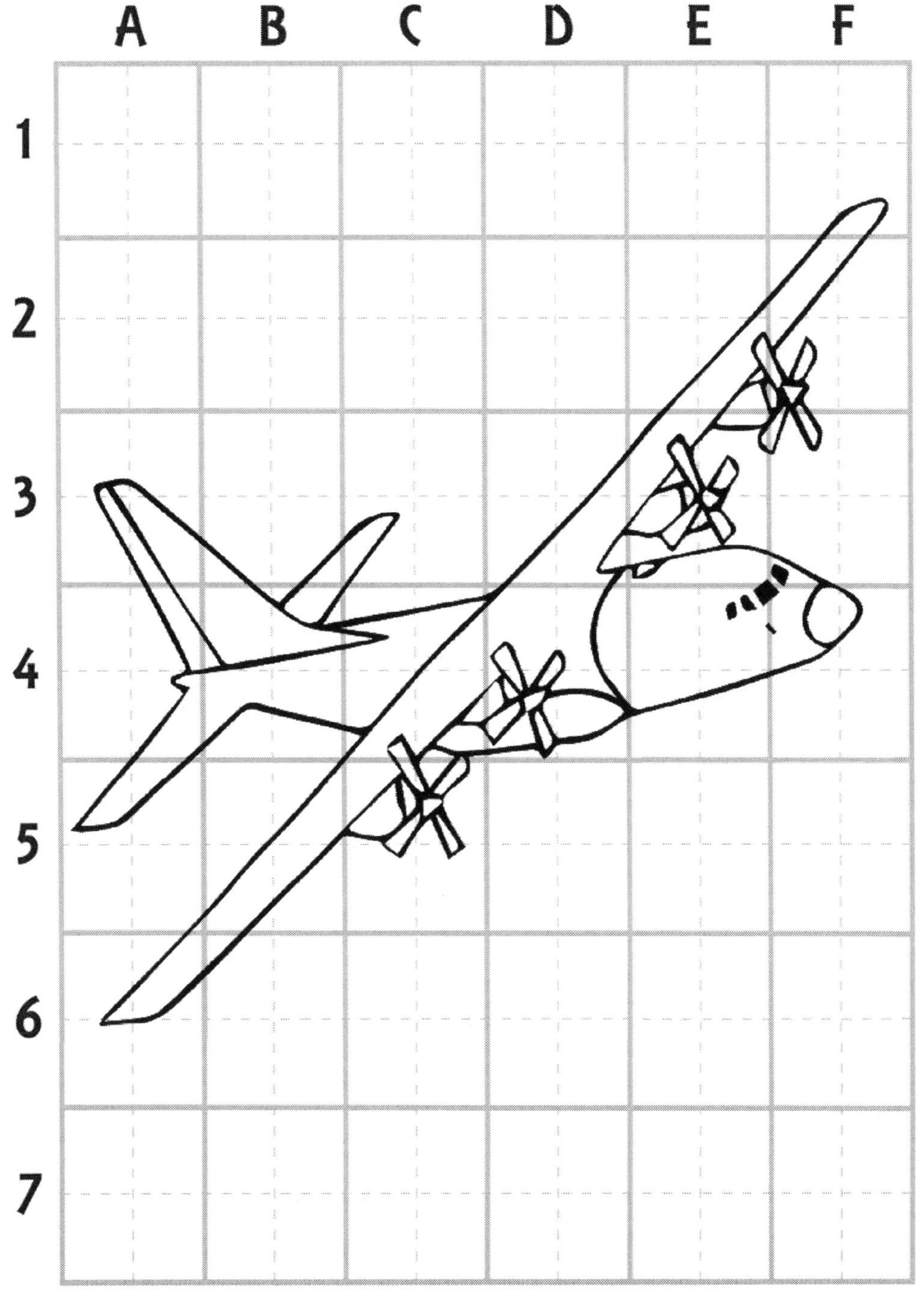
A
B
C
D
E
F
1
2
3
4
5
6
7

	A	B	C	D	E	F
1						
2						
3						
4						
5						
6						
7						

TRAINS

A
B
C
D
E
F
1
2
3
4
5
6
7

	A	B	C	D	E	F
1						
2						
3						
4						
5						
6						
7						

SHIPS

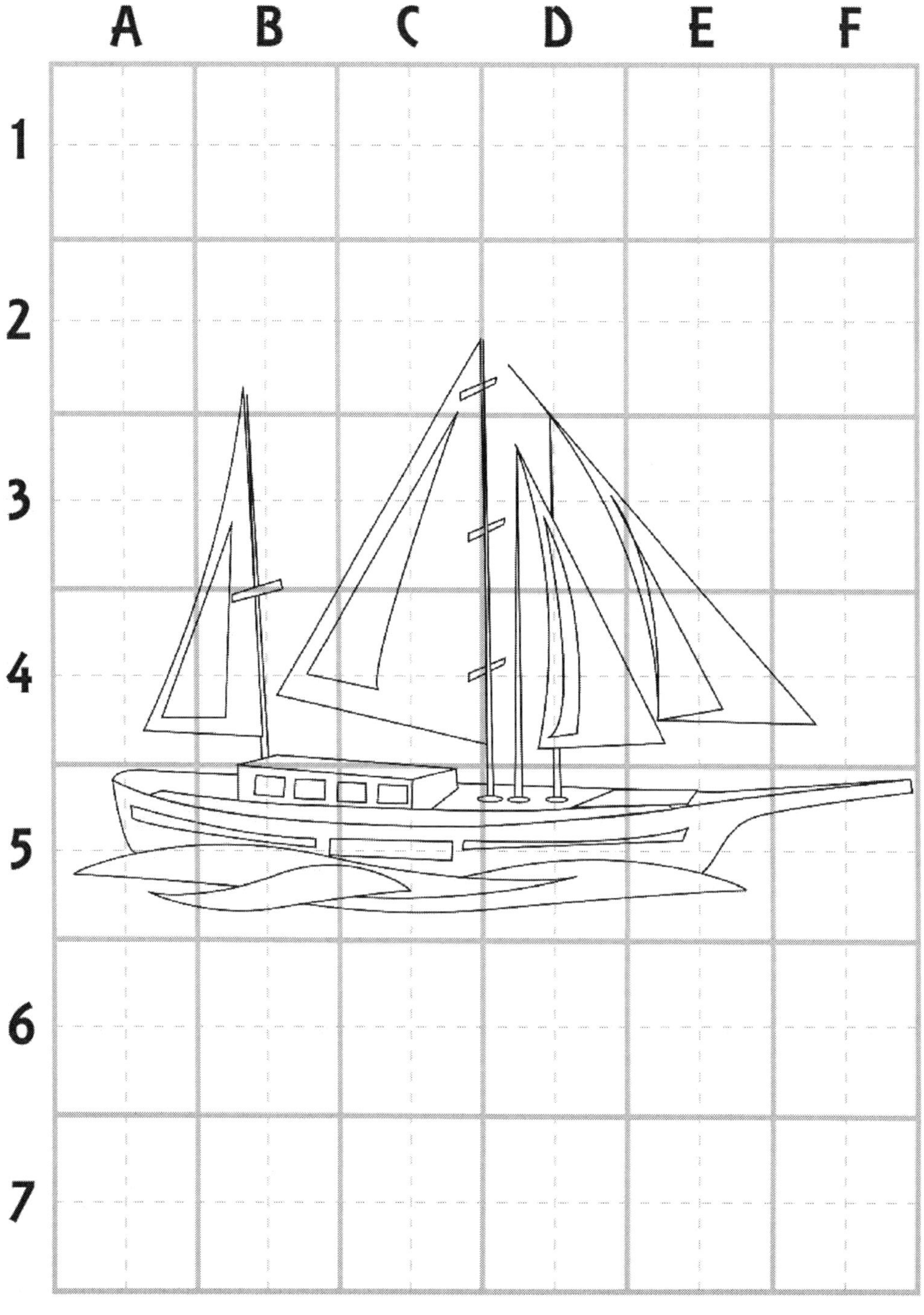
A
B
C
D
E
F
1
2
3
4
5
6
7

	A	B	C	D	E	F
1						
2						
3						
4						
5						
6						
7						

AIRPLANE

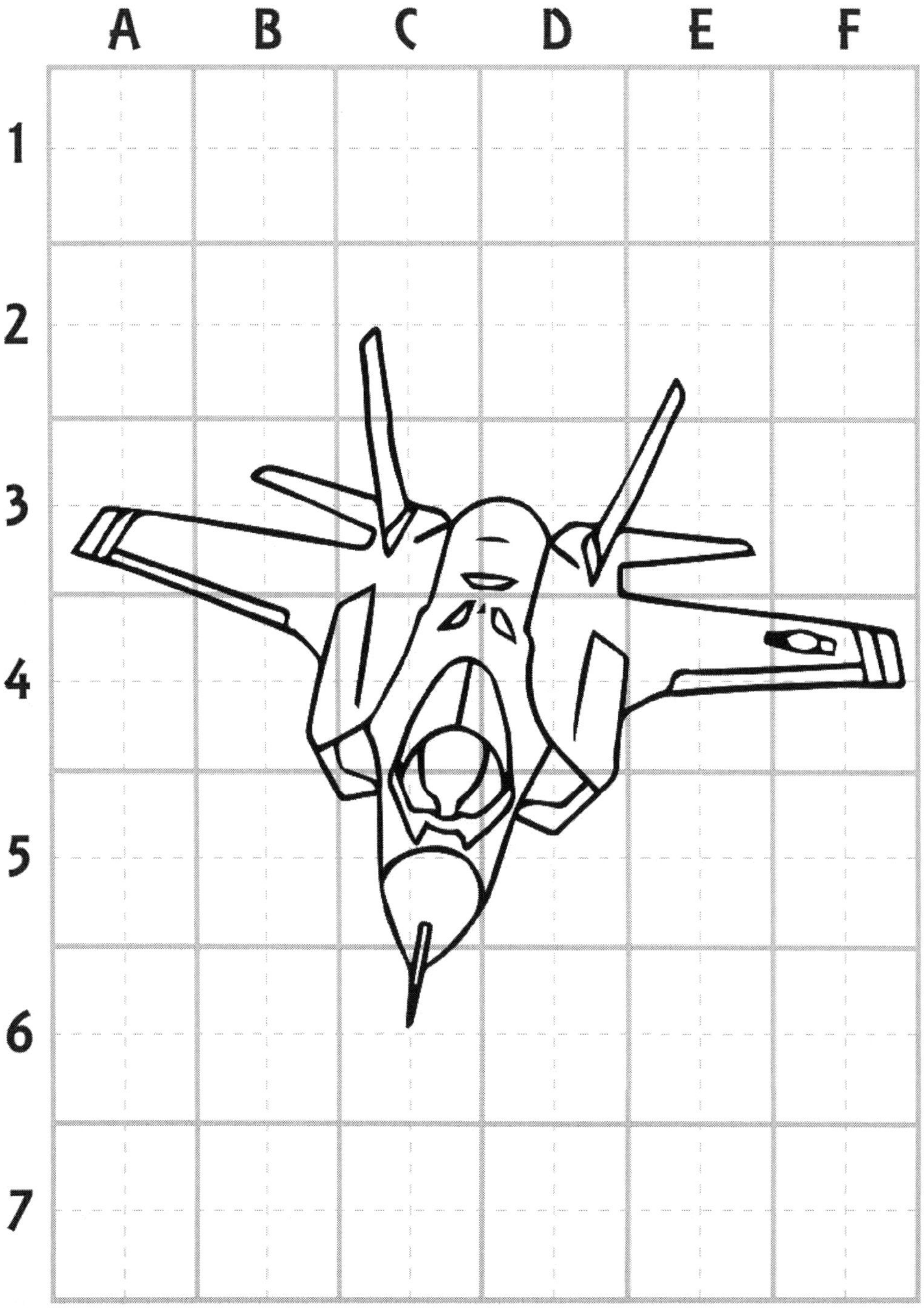
A
B
C
D
E
F
1
2
3
4
5
6
7

	A	B	C	D	E	F
1						
2						
3						
4						
5						
6						
7						

TRAINS

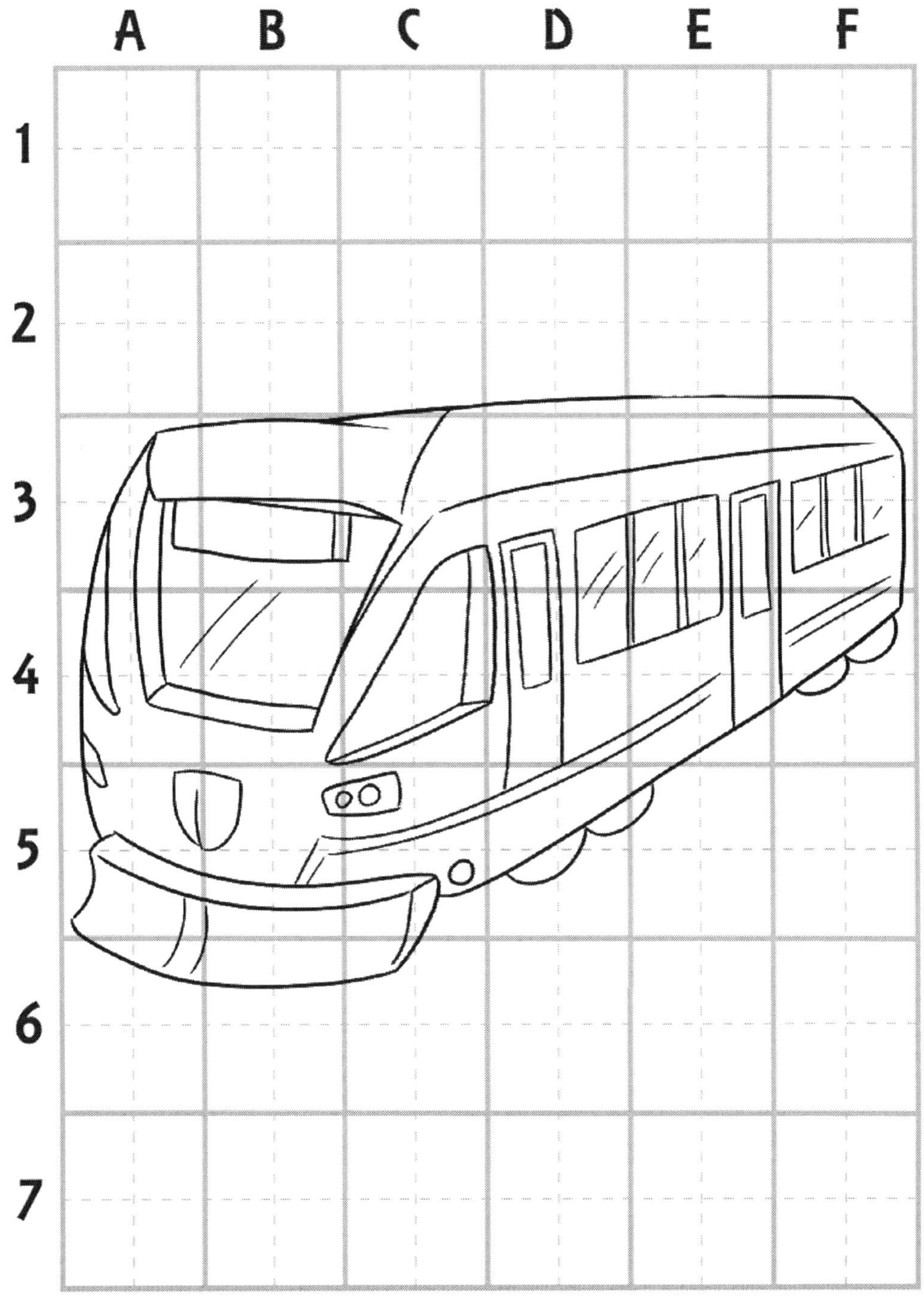
A B C D E F
1
2
3
4
5
6
7

	A	B	C	D	E	F
1						
2						
3						
4						
5						
6						
7						

SHIPS

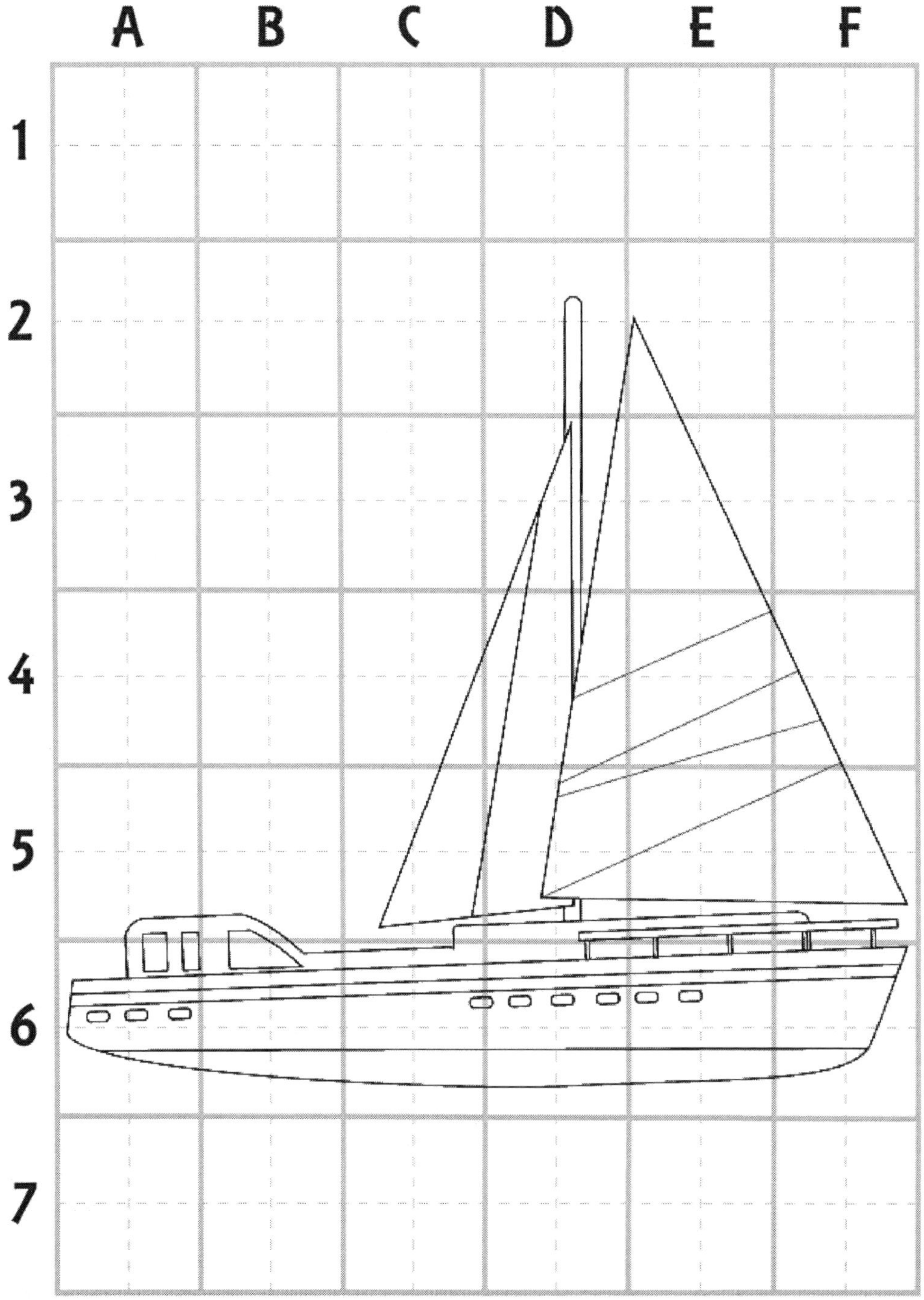
A
B
C
D
E
F
1
2
3
4
5
6
7

	A	B	C	D	E	F
1						
2						
3						
4						
5						
6						
7						

AIRPLANE

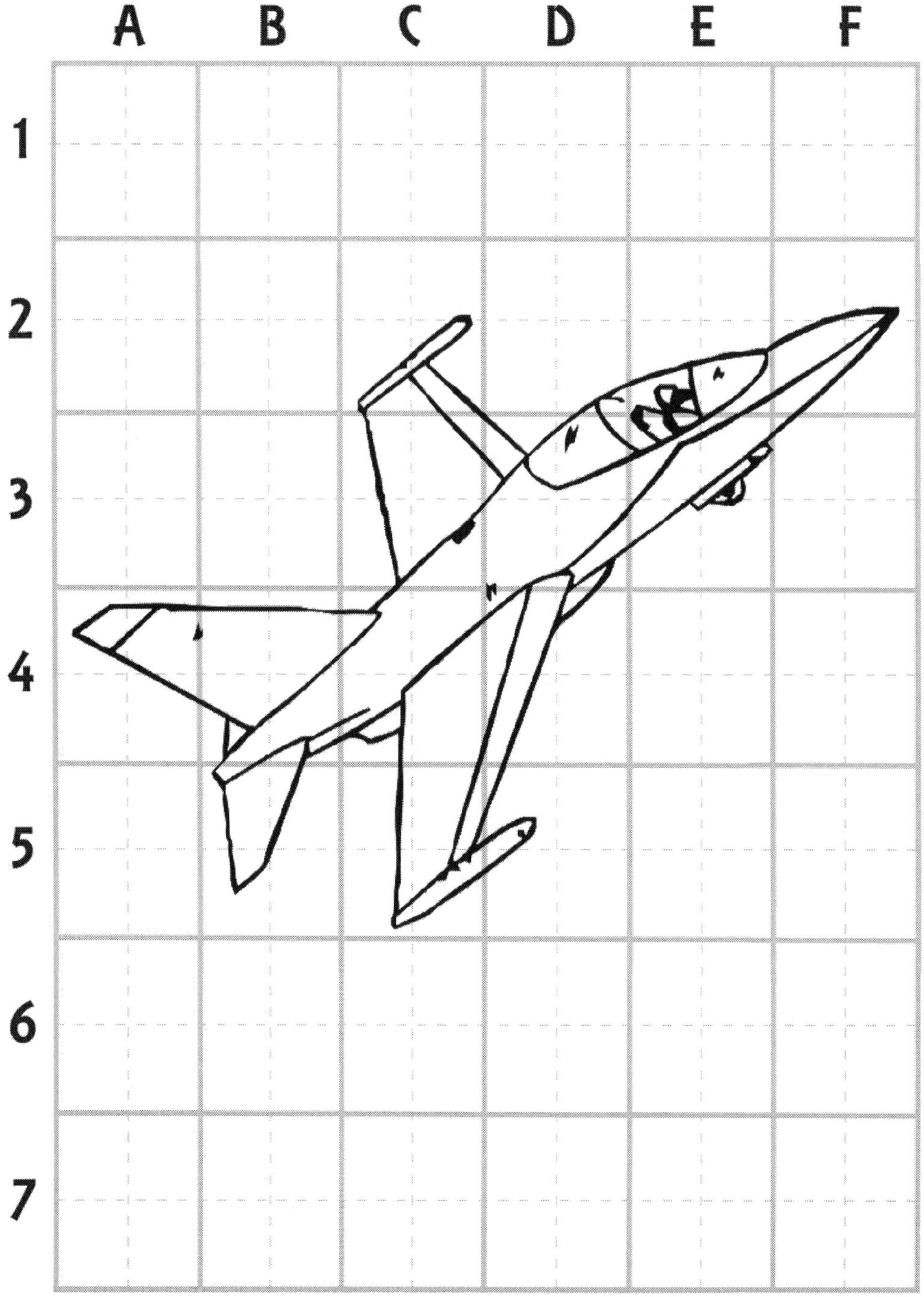
A
B
C
D
E
F
1
2
3
4
5
6
7

	A	B	C	D	E	F
1						
2						
3						
4						
5						
6						
7						

TRAINS

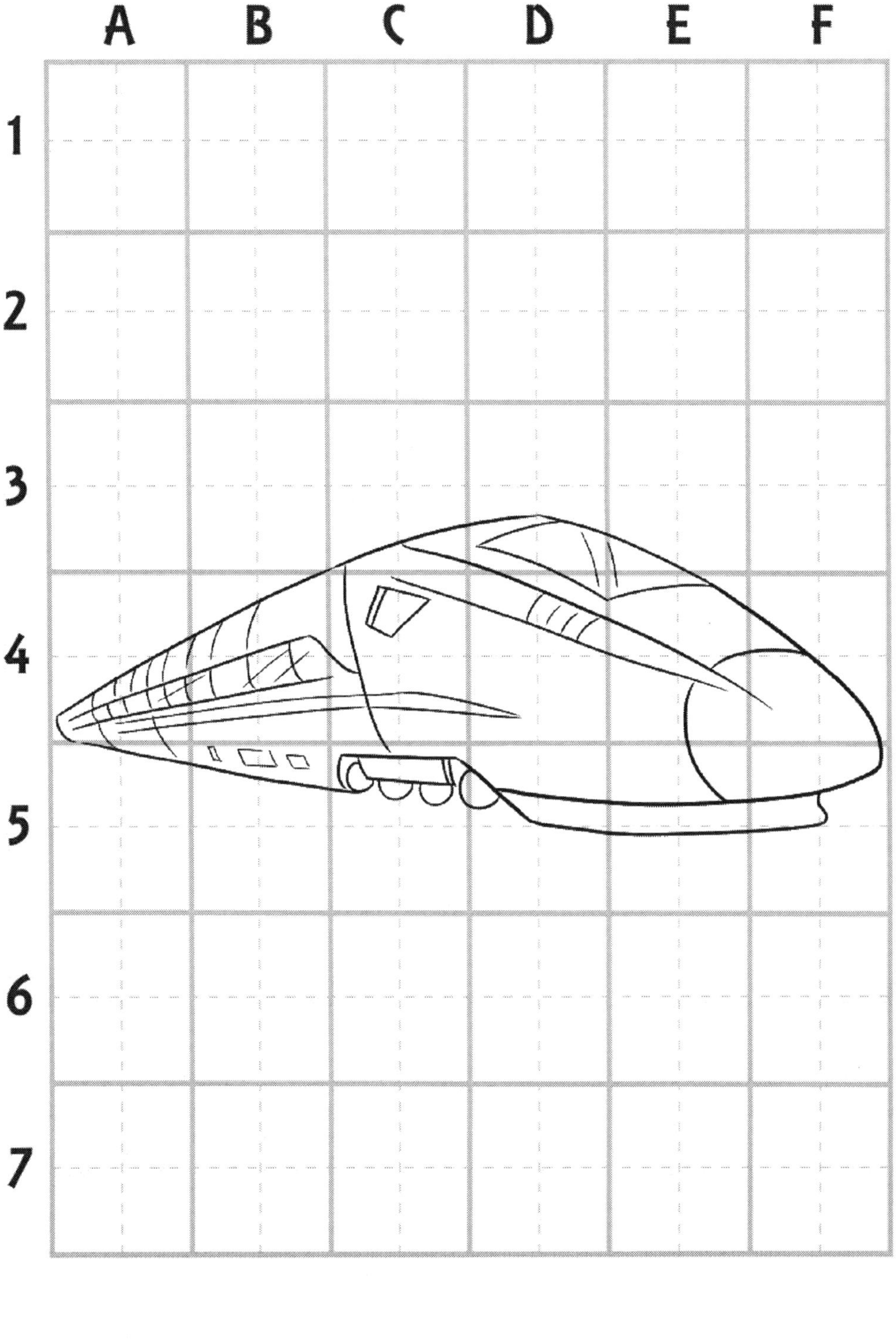
A
B
C
D
E
F
1
2
3
4
5
6
7

	A	B	C	D	E	F
1						
2						
3						
4						
5						
6						
7						

SHIPS

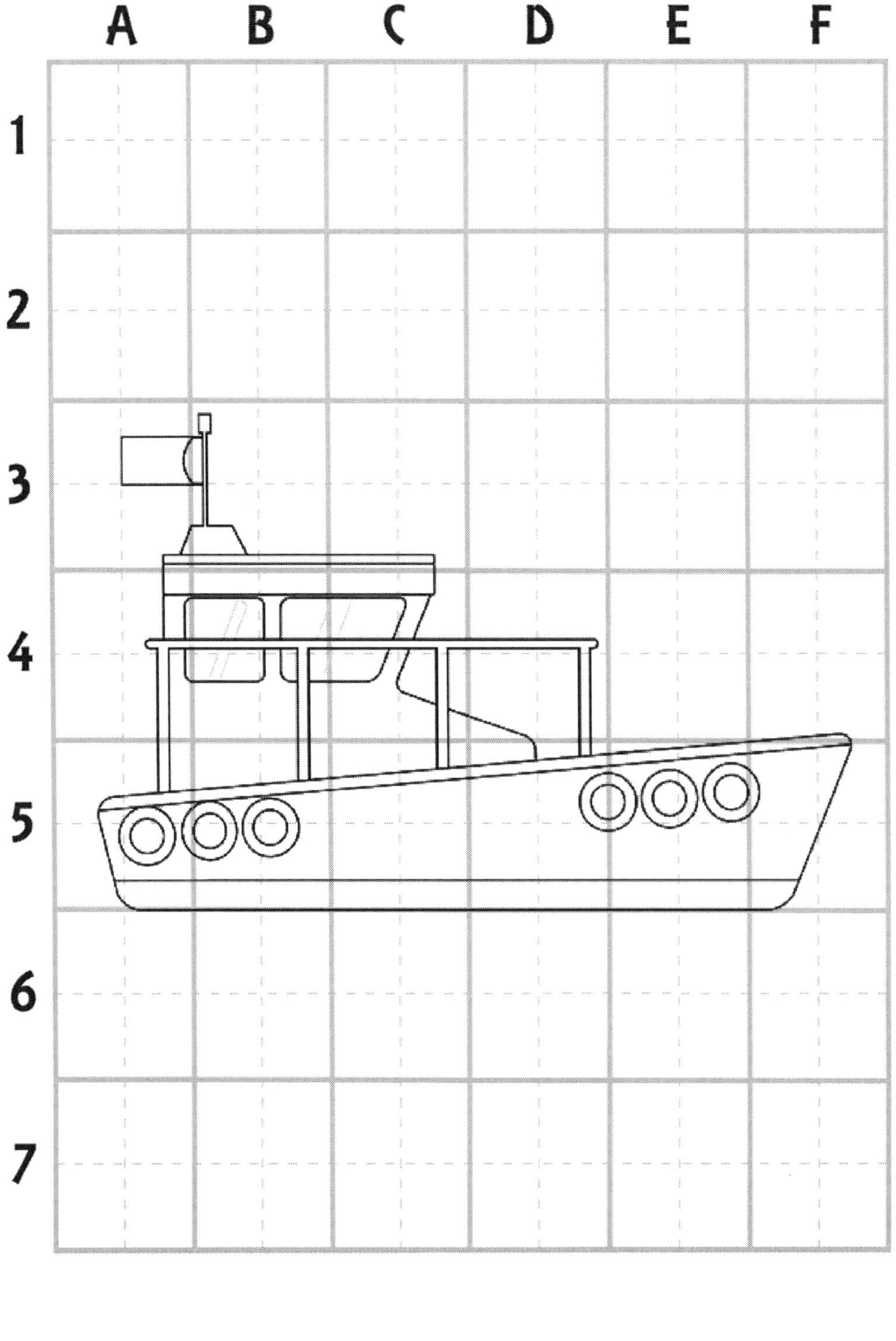
A
B
C
D
E
F
1
2
3
4
5
6
7

	A	B	C	D	E	F
1						
2						
3						
4						
5						
6						
7						

AIRPLANE

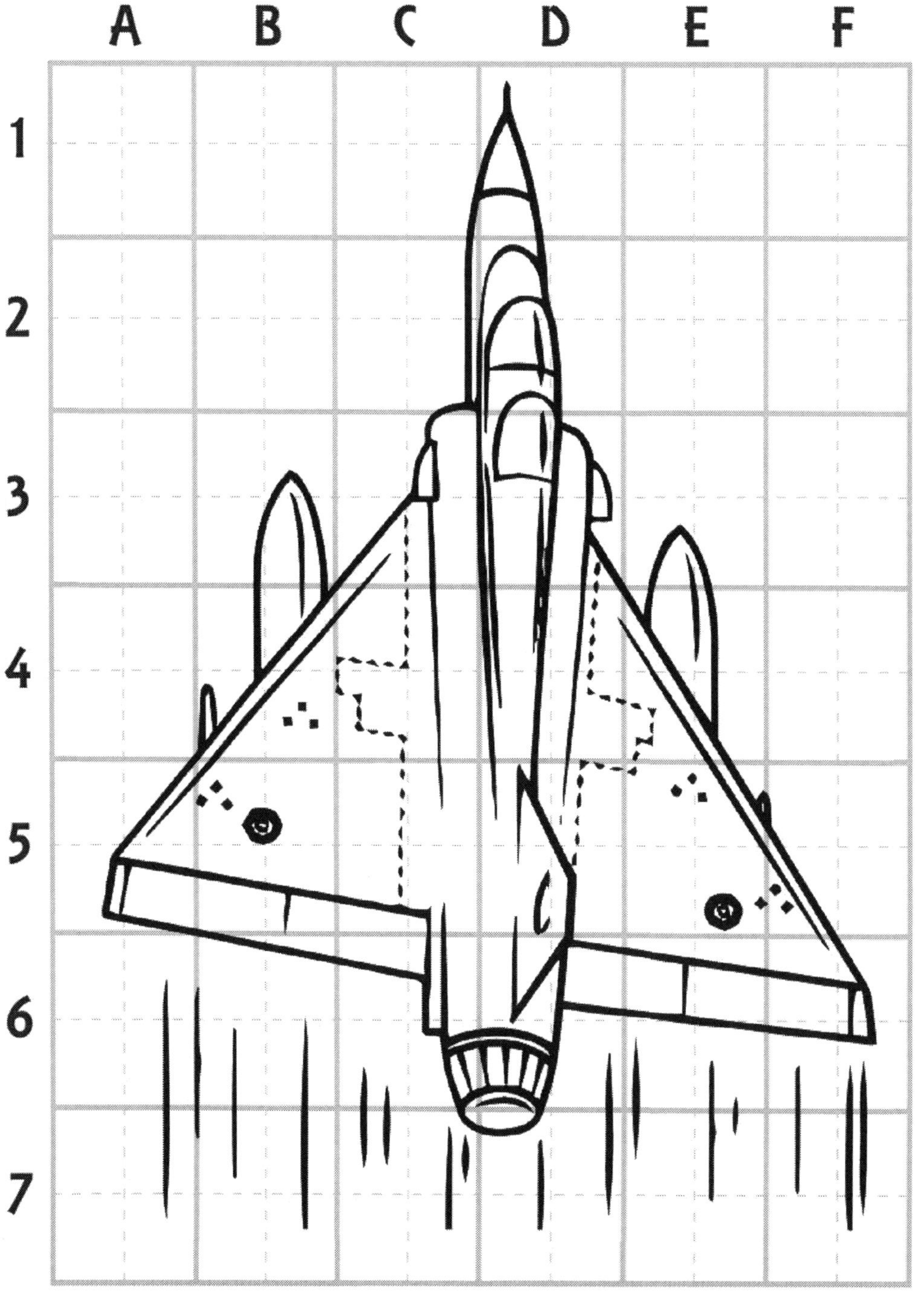
A
B
C
D
E
F
1
2
3
4
5
6
7

	A	B	C	D	E	F
1						
2						
3						
4						
5						
6						
7						

TRAINS

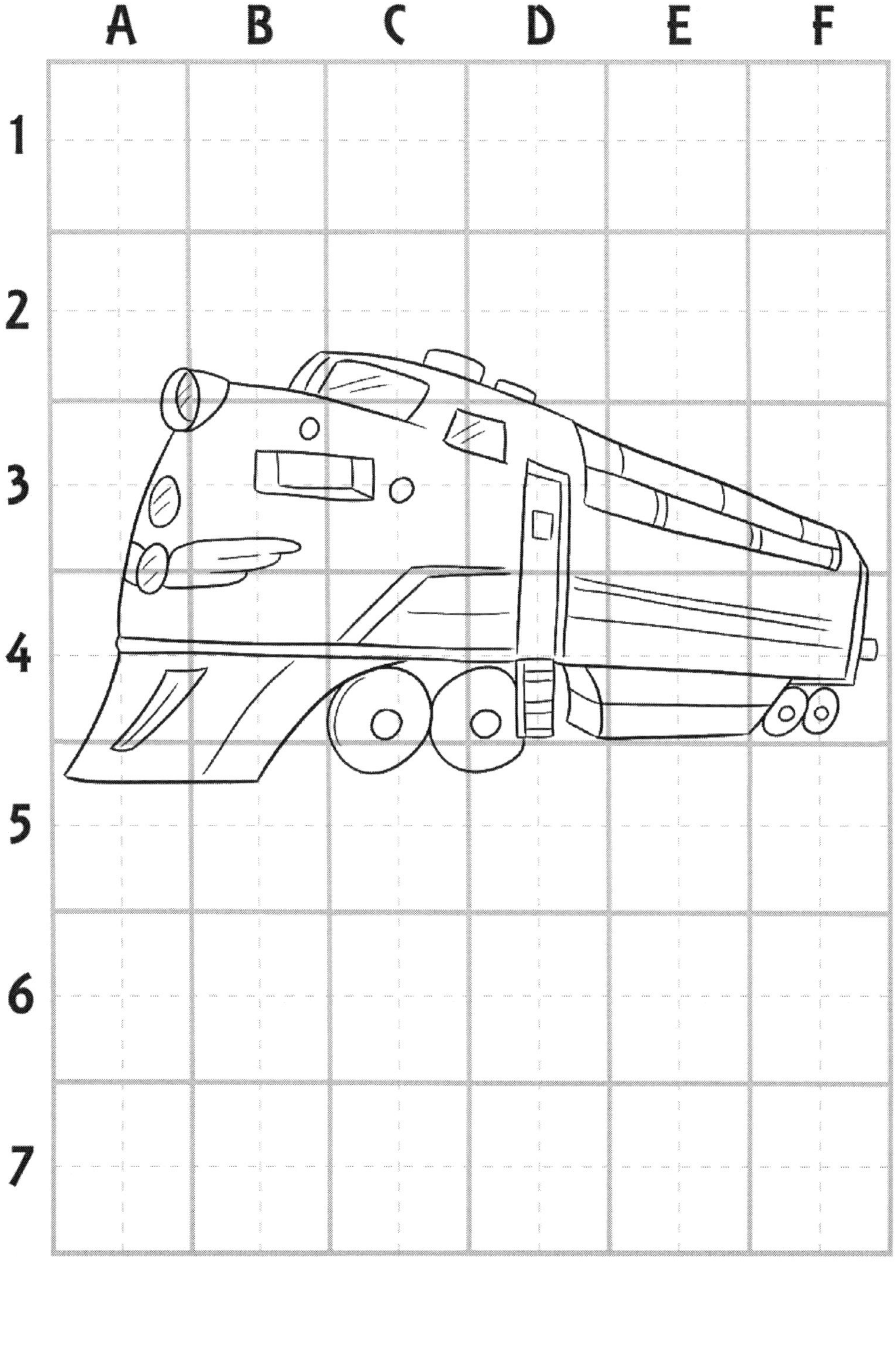
A
B
C
D
E
F
1
2
3
4
5
6
7

	A	B	C	D	E	F
1						
2						
3						
4						
5						
6						
7						

SHIPS

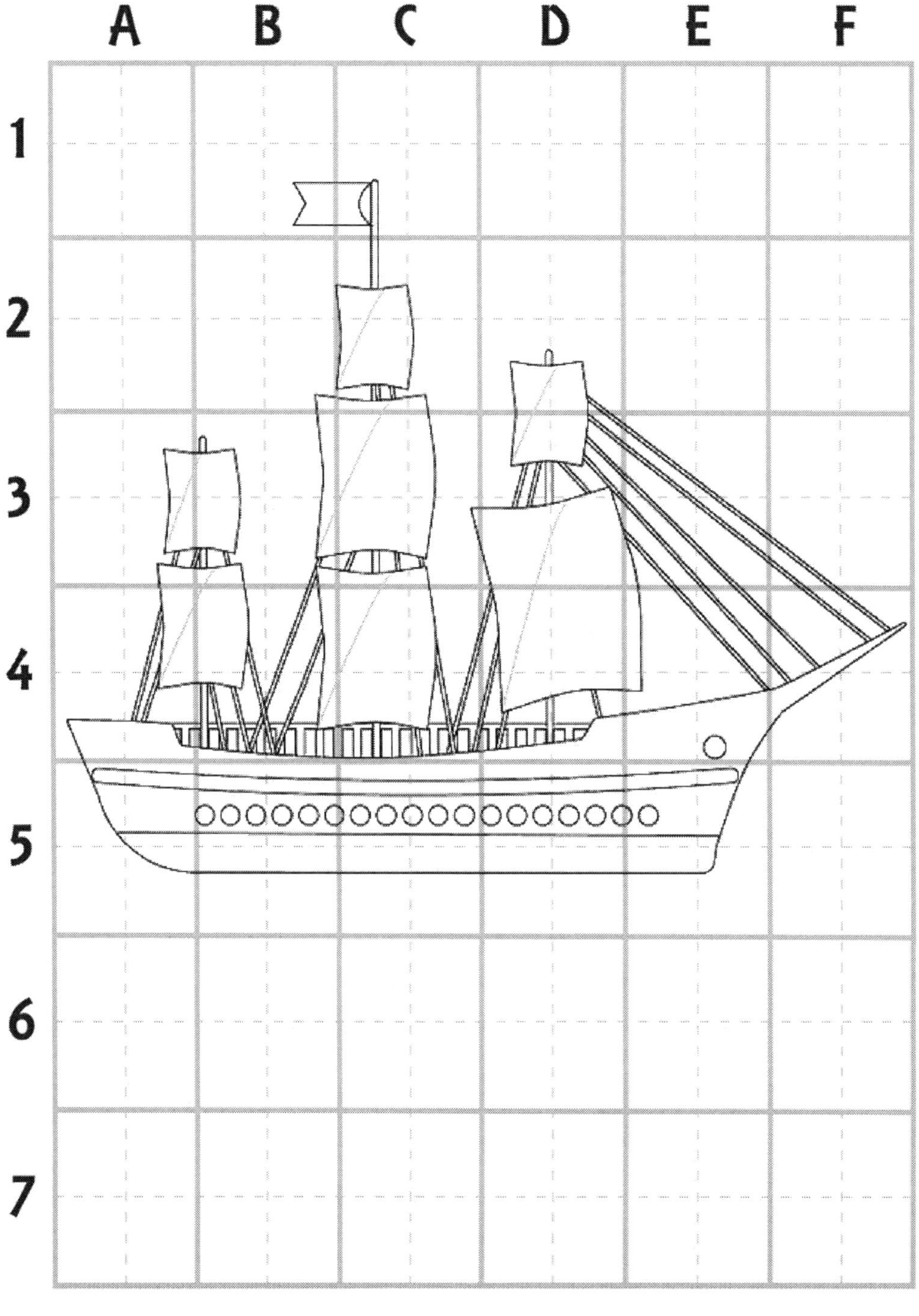
A
B
C
D
E
F
1
2
3
4
5
6
7

	A	B	C	D	E	F
1						
2						
3						
4						
5						
6						
7						

Congratulations
You are a great little artist

Thank you

We hope you enjoyed our book.

As a small family company, we are constantly trying to improve our work and your feedback is very important to us.

Please, let us know how you liked our book giving a rating and a review on the website of purchasing platform or at the email address mentioned below.

inspiringkidseducation@gmail.com

We would so appreciate it!

Printed in Great Britain
by Amazon

71548134R00043